26

FINANCIAL LITERACY

MAKING SMART MONEY CHOICES

By Moira Rose Donohue

CONTENT CONSULTANT
Dr. Linda Simpson, PhD, CFCS, CPFFE
Professor
Eastern Illinois University

Essential Library

An Imprint of Abdo Publishing | abdobooks.com

ABDOBOOKS.COM

Published by Abdo Publishing, a division of ABDO, PO Box 398166, Minneapolis, Minnesota 55439. Copyright © 2020 by Abdo Consulting Group, Inc. International copyrights reserved in all countries. No part of this book may be reproduced in any form without written permission from the publisher. Essential Library™ is a trademark and logo of Abdo Publishing.

Printed in the United States of America, North Mankato, Minnesota.
032019
092019

Cover Photo: Shutterstock Images
Interior Photos: iStockphoto, 5, 11, 17, 27, 28, 31, 37 (top right), 53, 55, 62, 68, 77, 83, 91; Light Field Studios/iStockphoto, 7, 23; Xi Xin Xing/iStockphoto, 15, 59; Larry St. Pierre/Shutterstock Images, 19; Red Line Editorial, 25, 48; Syda Productions/Shutterstock Images, 35; Anton Violin/Shutterstock Images, 37 (top left); Zerbor/iStockphoto, 37 (bottom left); Doubletree Studio/Shutterstock Images, 37 (bottom right); Shutterstock Images, 40, 67, 87; Andrey Popov/Shutterstock Images, 42; Way Home Studio/Shutterstock Images, 47; Nuthawut Somsuk/iStockphoto, 61; FatCamera/iStockphoto, 71; Sid Hastings/AP Images, 75; Luciano Mortula LGM/Shutterstock Images, 93; Alexandra Lakovleva/iStockphoto, 97

Editor: Alyssa Krekelberg
Series Designer: Colleen McLaren

LIBRARY OF CONGRESS CONTROL NUMBER: 2018965970

PUBLISHER'S CATALOGING-IN-PUBLICATION DATA

Names: Donohue, Moira Rose, author.
Title: Making smart money choices / by Moira Rose Donohue.
Description: Minneapolis, Minnesota: Abdo Publishing, 2020 | Series: Financial literacy | Includes online resources and index.
Identifiers: ISBN 9781532119132 (lib. bdg.) | ISBN 9781532173318 (ebook)
Subjects: LCSH: Saving and investment--Juvenile literature. | Personal finance--Juvenile literature. | Money supply--Juvenile literature.
Classification: DDC 332.024--dc23

So all readers may use the worksheets, please complete the exercises in your own notebook.

CONTENTS

CHAPTER ONE

EMPTY POCKETS

Terry glanced at his phone—the mall was closing in just 15 minutes. He placed his purchase on the glass countertop. It was a chess set fashioned out of onyx, coral, and marble. It was the perfect gift for his grandfather's birthday. Terry smiled to himself as he imagined his grandfather's face when he opened the present. Terry slipped the bills out of his wallet. The clerk counted them out and told him that he was short. The chess set was $89.72, and Terry had only given him $81. Terry thrust his hand into his pocket and felt around. Nothing in one pocket and only a few cents in the other. How could that be?

When he had come up with this idea a few weeks ago, he had asked his father how much a stone chess set would cost. His father thought it would be between $80 and $90. So Terry had then counted the money in his wallet and discovered he had $14.32. He knew he had two more allowances before the big day, so that

It's a good idea for people to know how much money they have before spending it.

IN THE RED

When businesses, individuals, or families are in the red, it means that they owe more money than they have. The phrase comes from the fact that bookkeepers, who are people hired to keep track of the income and expenses of businesses, used to enter debts or losses in red ink, and some still do. No one is quite sure why they used red ink. It may have been to make the entries stand out from items listed in black ink. The first known use of the phrase to mean someone was in financial trouble was in a book published in 1907 about money and investments.

was $20 more. But he still needed around $55, plus a little extra for sales tax.

To earn the rest, he offered to do chores around the house. He took the trash out every night for two weeks and earned $10, and he babysat his little sister for another $25. He mowed the lawn twice, earning him another $20, and then offered to cut the neighbor's lawn for $10. Terry didn't keep track of how much he was making—he just stuck the money into his wallet. On Monday, after he got his last allowance, he took out all the money—bills and coins—and discovered he had $99.32. He ran his hand around the sofa cushions and found two quarters. Then he peeked under the bed and, amid the dust bunnies, a dirty sock, and an old

Doing chores can be one way for teenagers to earn extra money.

pizza crust, found one more quarter. He had $100.07—more than enough for the chess set. So where was the money now?

Could it have fallen out of his wallet when he bought that pretzel and lemonade? If he had dropped it, somebody probably picked it up and it was gone for good. But then he remembered that the snack had cost $6.76. He opened the calculator on his phone and punched in numbers. He should have $93.31. Had he bought anything else since last Monday? Well, he had handed his buddy Josh $5 for the pizza they ordered when they were playing video games on Wednesday. He racked his brain, trying to remember anything else. Yes, he had bought a school spirit hat for $7 that afternoon. Although he hadn't really wanted it, everyone else was getting hats and he didn't want to stand out. When he subtracted those purchases, he came up short.

The clerk raised an eyebrow and asked Terry whether he was going to buy the chess set. Terry was embarrassed as he told the clerk that he didn't have enough cash, and the clerk then asked whether he had a debit card, a credit card, or a check. The clerk added that there was an automated teller machine (ATM) by the food court.

Terry wasn't sure what the clerk was talking about. He had a bank account, but he'd never withdrawn money from it. His parents had set up the account to use for cash

RETAIL ENVIRONMENTS

Modern malls started popping up in the mid-1900s. Today, Minnesota is home to one of the largest malls in the United States, the Mall of America, which stretches for millions of square feet and even has amusement park rides. Teenagers today still shop at malls. But they also shop at thrift stores and discount stores, such as Marshalls. And online shopping is popular. In 2016, 33 percent of teenagers said they preferred to shop online rather than in stores.[1]

TYPES OF MONETARY GIFTS

Adults sometimes give young people different types of monetary gifts, such as cash or checks, for special occasions. Young people should take a little time to decide whether to spend the gift all at once or save it for something else later. Teens also frequently receive gift cards. Sometimes, these cards can be used only in the store or restaurant listed on the card. It's a good idea to look at the back because sometimes these cards can be used at related businesses. And some have expiration dates, so it's smart to check.

Adults also sometimes give young people savings bonds. A savings bond is the safest form of investment because it's backed by the federal government. They work like this: a $5,000 savings bond costs $2,500 to buy. If cashed at its maturity date—usually 20 years—it will be worth $5,000—double what the purchaser paid for it.[2]

gifts from family members to save up for college. And he had savings bonds that his aunt gave him every year for his birthday, but they were tucked away somewhere in his dresser drawer. Besides, he wasn't sure how to spend them. And he had no credit or debit cards. Just then, Terry's dad tapped him on the shoulder and asked whether he was ready to go. Terry explained his dilemma. His dad agreed to give Terry the money he needed, but he said it would come out of Terry's next allowance. And he said it was time that Terry learned how to make good money choices. Terry suppressed

HOW LIQUID ARE YOU?

In economic terms, *liquidity* refers to how much money a person has in the form of cash or other liquid assets. Cash is generally accepted everywhere. And sometimes merchants such as food truck operators or craft vendors accept only cash. Liquid assets are things such as checking accounts or savings bonds that can be sold or converted to cash very easily. Real estate, a diamond ring, or a painting may have great value, but such items are not liquid. However, a paycheck that can be cashed at a bank is.

a groan, knowing his dad could drone on about such things. But he thought that his dad was probably right.

KEEPING TRACK OF SPENDING

Terry had done a commendable job of saving up more than enough money for his grandfather's present. At first, he even had a little money left over. He could have afforded any one of his small purchases. But what he failed to do was to keep track of his spending, either by writing down his expenses and subtracting them from his total or simply by counting his cash after each purchase. Alternatively, he could have stuffed $90 into a separate envelope or corner of his wallet to make sure he didn't spend it.

Being in debt can cause people a lot of stress.

Terry's case of not keeping track of his money was a small problem, and his father came to his rescue. But as people get older, this money habit can become a more serious problem and can even lead to debt. The 2009 US census found that 69 percent of all households were in debt and that Americans were spending $1.33 for every $1 earned.[3] Data reported by the Federal Reserve Board in 2017 found that more than 77 percent of all families have some debt.[4]

Various financial advisers offer different suggestions about how to manage money. But there are several strategies that are recommended repeatedly. First, people should understand why they're overspending and then avoid the triggers. Triggers can be boredom, being upset, and peer pressure—like what Terry experienced when he bought the school spirit hat he didn't want. The second strategy is to keep track of all spending, because small purchases add up. Terry found that out the hard way. Creating a budget is a third critical strategy. Creating a budget involves setting SMART financial goals. These goals are specific, measurable, attainable, relevant, and time bound. Finally, most money consultants agree that staying out of debt and not abusing credit cards is fundamental to making smart money choices and managing money in a healthy way.

WHERE IS YOUR MONEY?

Before you can begin to take charge and make smart money decisions, you need to figure out exactly how much money you have. Use this worksheet to help you track where your money is and calculate the total amount. Look through all the places you keep your money.

Cash in your wallet and pockets: _____

Cash in a piggy bank or coin jar: _____

Cash stashed in other places in your room: _____

Money in a checking account: _____

Money in a savings account: _____

Savings bonds: _____

Any other money: _____

Now add it all up and figure out your total:

_____

CHAPTER TWO

NEEDS, WANTS, AND OPPORTUNITY COSTS

E veryone in the world shares the same basic needs: food, clothing, and shelter. In different cultures and climates, these needs are met in different ways. For example, people who live in Panama wear different clothing than those who live in an area with a different climate, such as Iceland. Shelter, clothing, and food will also vary depending on how much money a person has. But meeting these basic needs, wherever people live, costs money—and that's why it's so important.

The money that teens get through gifts, allowances, or earnings can often be used for things known as wants. Sports cars, video games, designer handbags, and trendy sneakers are examples of wants.

Financial experts generally agree that it's a mistake for people to purchase something they want before

One example of a need is food.

HOW MONEY IS MADE

The US Mint produces coins. Paper money, however, is made by the Bureau of Engraving and Printing (BEP), which is part of the US Treasury Department. The BEP prints bills in the following denominations: $1, $5, $10, $20, $50, and $100. These bills have limited life spans. One-dollar bills usually last approximately 5.8 years. Larger-denomination bills can last up to 15 years. When the condition of a bill is no longer good, it is taken out of circulation and destroyed.

they have enough money to pay for the things they need. Consider this hypothetical situation: a parent might give her child a certain amount of money each week to pay for lunch. That child needs to eat lunch. But he decides to spend all the money on a movie and popcorn after class one day. The child has chosen a want over a need. And that choice will likely create problems—his stomach is going to rumble like a truck engine every afternoon for the rest of the week. The smart money choice is for the child to plan ahead and figure out how to get the money to pay for the outing to the movies by doing chores, working for a neighbor, or saving up his allowance. If he can't, the wise decision is to

Going to a movie might be a fun way to hang out with friends, but people should consider the cost.

MISSED OPPORTUNITY

Teenagers can use the opportunity cost analysis for big decisions, such as whether to go to a state university or a more expensive private college. Even governments use opportunity cost analysis. A county government with limited money has to decide how to spend it. Should it build a new library or hire more people on the police force? First, county officials compare the actual cost of building the library with the actual cost of hiring more police workers for the year. But then they must consider what is lost by choosing to add a library rather than protect citizens with more police officers. Sometimes this decision needs to take into account the values of the community.

meet his needs (lunch) rather than his wants (the movie).

OPPORTUNITY COST

What if someone has enough money to meet basic needs but not enough to satisfy all of his wants? Economists are people who study how individuals and businesses spend money. They have identified a way to help make tough money choices. They call it determining the opportunity cost. When people make a choice, they give up something. The value of the alternative choice—or, in the case of more than one alternative, the one with the next-highest value—is called the opportunity cost.

Being on a sports team can be a big time commitment.

Consider a student who has the chance to play on either a regular sports team or a higher-level sports team, such as a traveling soccer team. The traveling soccer team has games almost every Saturday, some of which are away games. The regular team plays on Friday nights at nearby fields. This leaves the student's Saturday mornings free to babysit routinely for her neighbor. Which should she choose?

First, there is the actual cost of being on the traveling soccer team. The girl's parents have said they will pay the soccer club dues and will drive her to practice and the games. But they said that she needs to pay for the soccer uniform, which is $75.

However, the opportunity cost is more than that. Because most of the traveling team games are a long distance away, the student will be busy most of the day on Saturday. That will require her to give up her regular babysitting job on Saturday morning.

The opportunity cost for playing soccer is $75, plus the income she'll lose by not being able to babysit on Saturday mornings for $20, which, multiplied over the 12-week season, is $240. That's a cost of $315. But she'll be able to hone her soccer skills and have the enjoyment and status of playing on a better team. Using this opportunity cost analysis can help a person make an informed, smart money choice between two or more wants.

A LOOK AT OPPORTUNITY COSTS

Think of two things you want to do. For example, you might have to choose between going to a concert or staying home and playing a video game with your best friend. Make a list of the opportunity costs associated with each choice. Then, pick which activity you would rather do.

Activity	What did you gain?	What else could you do with your time or money?

CHAPTER THREE

SMART WAYS TO GET MONEY

Money helps people buy things they want. So how do they get money for their wants, and how do they decide what to spend it on? According to a 2018 survey, approximately 70 percent of people age four to 14 in the United States receive some form of allowance—a regular, often weekly, payment from their parents.[1] How much someone collects depends on the person's age and the family's financial situation, but the average allowance is around $8 each week.[2] Some parents tie allowances to chores such as cleaning bedrooms, doing laundry, or looking after pets. Others provide allowances that are unrelated to chores. No matter how allowance is given, many parents ask that their children budget the

Some people think an allowance will help teach teens how to manage money.

allowance they receive and expect them to pay for their personal expenses during the week.

ALLOWANCES

Getting an allowance is a good way to learn about smart money management. It teaches young people the value of things they want. It makes them appreciate how hard it is to get money and therefore how hard it is to part with it. It can help them identify when items aren't worth the price being asked. If it took someone a week to get a $10 allowance, is it worth spending half of it on one fancy cup of coffee? It can also help them understand, for instance, that there is a cost associated with convenience, such as paying more for a sandwich from a shop instead of fixing a sandwich at home. Handling a weekly allowance encourages people to budget their money.

A 2017 survey asked teens what they spend their allowance money on. Food is the number one item, followed by clothing and cars. In addition to allowances, many teens get money for birthdays or other special occasions. That accounts for an average of $43.94 a year, according to the same survey.[3] And some teens are rewarded with additional money for getting good grades or behaving well. Allowance and gift money can be put aside for a special present for

AVERAGE ALLOWANCE[4]

In 2017, the amount of allowance people received each week increased with age.

Age

Age	Amount
Four	$3.76
Five	$4.21
Six	$5.24
Seven	$6.69
Eight	$7.24
Nine	$7.80
Ten	$8.10
Eleven	$9.40
Twelve	$9.85
Thirteen	$10.79
Fourteen	$12.26

$0 $2 $4 $6 $8 $10 $12 $14

Amount

someone. Some teens save up their allowances to buy luxury items, such as a designer-brand purse or a video game. Saving allowance or birthday money for a big-ticket purchase requires patience. But there are additional ways teens can acquire more money.

EARNING THROUGH CHORES

Often, an allowance is not enough to meet all of someone's money goals. When that happens, the smart thing to do is to look for other ways to earn money. One way to get money to meet these goals is by performing common household chores for a price, beyond any that are tied to an allowance. Some of the most common chores for extra money include providing childcare for siblings or other young children, washing or folding clothes, taking care of pets, mowing the lawn, taking out the trash, making meals, and washing dishes. Some of these chores are one-time jobs, such as babysitting on a special occasion. Others are repetitive, such as taking the trash out twice a week. The fee usually reflects the difficulty of the chore and how often it's done.

Doing chores can teach young people basic life skills, such as how to do laundry or cook. And sometimes these chores can help teens learn what kind of job they might want in the future. For example, if a person likes caring for young children, perhaps this could lead to a future career in childcare or teaching. Or if a person likes mowing the lawn and working in the yard, maybe he or she would enjoy landscape

Helping neighbors can be one way to earn extra money.

Part-time jobs can teach teens the value of money.

work or another job outdoors. Experience gained by performing chores can be useful in future jobs.

EMPLOYMENT AND ENTREPRENEURIAL EFFORTS

When a young person has a certain financial goal, such as saving for college, it's smart to find ways to earn money to achieve that goal. Teenagers who are 14 or older can work in certain paid jobs. To protect young workers, federal and state governments have identified jobs that are too dangerous for people under the age of 18. But there are still a number of jobs that

CHILD LABOR LAWS

Although children have worked throughout history, child labor became particularly hazardous and brutal during the Industrial Revolution. This was a time of rapid industrial development starting in the late 1700s caused by new machinery. In 1900, 18 percent of the workforce was under age 16.[5] Children worked long hours in dangerous factories for very little money. Moreover, these children were unable to get an education. The United States was slow to adopt reforms to protect them. But during the Great Depression (1929–1939), adults were so desperate to get work themselves that they were willing to keep children out of the workforce. So in 1938, Congress passed the Fair Labor Standards Act, which included limitations on the hours that children could work and restricted the types of industries, such as mining, that could employ children under the age of 16.

teens can do, usually on a part-time basis for those under 16. For example, people 14 and older can work as camp counselors, as lifeguards, on golf courses, in retail stores, at movie theaters, and in offices. However, in each paycheck the government may deduct certain amounts from wages to pay for taxes, Social Security, and health-care programs. It's a smart idea for teens to keep track of how much money they are actually making.

Some teens venture outside of the standard work world to try to earn money. They are called entrepreneurs—people who start a business and

WHAT JOBS PAY

The earning potential of a career may affect a person's career choice. For example, according to the Bureau of Labor Statistics, in 2017 an average salary for an elementary school teacher was around $60,830. For people working in landscaping or groundskeeping, the average salary was around $29,700, and a chef made around $49,650 each year.[6] In 2018, jobs in the health-care industry, such as a physician, and the technology field, such as a software developer, paid the best. People in these jobs can have a salary of more than $100,000.[7]

assume the risk of running it. Some young entrepreneurs offer services to neighbors for a fee. These services include childcare, dog walking, and lawn mowing and other yard work. Sometimes young people take classes through community centers, such as classes in cardiopulmonary resuscitation (CPR), so they can learn emergency skills to make themselves more desirable in jobs such as childcare. To market the business, strategies include hanging posters, passing out flyers, placing notices on bulletin boards, and using online advertising. Young people with special skills in academics, a musical instrument, or art can offer to tutor young children. How much do they charge? The normal rate depends on where they live and the difficulty of the service

Taking care of pets is a big responsibility.

ENTREPRENEUR SUPERSTAR

Some teens have taken entrepreneurial ideas to a higher level. At age 13, Rachel Zietz, a lacrosse player, was frustrated with the quality and price of lacrosse products. Most players used a backyard lacrosse rebounder—a type of mesh practice wall. But Rachel thought that the backyard rebounders were not of high-enough quality. So she went to a program for young entrepreneurs and founded her own business to make and sell a better rebounder and a stronger practice goal net. Today she is the CEO of her company, Gladiator Lacrosse.

involved, so doing a little research is a good idea.

Selling products is another way to make extra money. The traditional summer neighborhood lemonade stand is a popular choice, but people should investigate city permits before pursuing this plan. People who can bake or make craft projects, such as jewelry or scarves, can sell their creations. They can set up stands in their neighborhood.

In setting a price, the expenses—the cost of the supplies—should be taken into account. The actual profit is only the money made that exceeds the expenses.

ADD UP YOUR INCOME

List all your sources of income for a sample month.

- Allowance: _____
- Chores: _____
- Rewards (for grades, etc.): _____
- Gifts (on average): _____
- Outside jobs in the neighborhood: _____
- Paid employment (after deductions): _____
- Sales and other entrepreneurial endeavors (after expenses): _____
- Other: _____

Now add it up.

Total: _____

Do you think your income can support your way of living? Why or why not?

_____
_____
_____
_____
_____
_____

CHAPTER FOUR

SMART PLACES TO KEEP MONEY

O nce people have figured out how to get money, they need to know where to keep it. While some people tuck money in piggy banks or stash cash in envelopes or coin jars, most Americans have at least one bank account. In the 1964 Walt Disney movie *Mary Poppins*, bankers sing the praises of "tuppence, prudently, thriftily, frugally, invested in the bank."[1] And as young people get older, they want to put their tuppence (two cents) in a bank account, too.

It's generally a smart choice to put money in a bank. That way it won't get lost and it can earn interest. Also, an insured bank account is safe and gives a person additional ways to pay for things such as a debit card. But the terms that banks use can be confusing, so it's a good idea to understand how banks work.

It's not smart for people to leave large amounts of cash lying around. Putting it in a bank can keep people's money more secure.

SMART MONEY CHOICES AND BANKS

Banks keep people's money safe. In the United States, an individual's money is insured, or protected, by the federal government up to a certain amount—$250,000 per person per bank in 2018.[2] That means that if anything happens to the bank, including a bank robbery, the Federal Deposit Insurance Corporation (FDIC) will pay customers their money. Because the US government insures banks, it has a strong incentive to regulate and examine them to make sure they don't make bad loans or other risky investments with insured funds. And banks are not permitted to lend out all the money they take in. They must keep a certain percentage of the money as reserves and a certain amount in the vault. This is known as vault cash.

HERE, PIGGY

The term *piggy bank* doesn't come from anything relating to a pig. In the Middle Ages, people made dishes and pots out of orange-colored clay. It was called *pygg*. When they had extra money, they dropped it into a pot made out of pygg. These became known as pygg pots or pygg banks. Over time, the word *pygg* became *pig*, and eventually someone designed one to look like a pig.

BANKING CYCLE

Bankers don't stick the money customers give them into their steel vaults. Instead, the bank uses the money to make car loans, home loans, and loans to businesses. These loans are paid back with interest, which is a percentage of the loan amount paid to the bank for each month it's borrowed. This is how the bank earns money. The bank, in turn, pays a smaller amount of interest to the customers who have placed their money in bank accounts. In reality, the money deposited in a bank is a loan to the bank.

People put money into savings accounts.

Banks loan money to businesses and people.

The bank pays interest to people with savings accounts.

People who get the loan pay the bank interest on it.

Having a bank account is both a smart and a convenient choice. With bank accounts, people know where their money is and how much they have. Usually, banks allow customers to set up online banking so they can check their balance from a phone or computer at any time. Depending on the type of account a person chooses, he or she can access money in several ways. So it's important that the person know what kind of bank account is the smart choice for him or her.

Banks offer various kinds of accounts. The main types of accounts are checking and savings. For people who want to be able to write checks, pay bills, or withdraw cash regularly, the smart choice is usually a checking account. To save money and earn a higher interest rate, most people choose some type of savings account, such as a money market

HISTORY OF THE FDIC

The FDIC was created in 1933. The United States was in the Great Depression after the stock market crashed in 1929. Over the next few years, a large number of banks closed because they had made poor investments. Congress passed laws to control what banks could do with deposits. To calm the nation and instill confidence in the banks, Congress set up the deposit insurance system in 1934, run by the FDIC.

deposit account (MMDA) or a certificate of deposit (CD). These accounts pay higher interest. But they may require a certain minimum balance, and they restrict the number or method of withdrawals of money. A banker will be able to tell people what kind of account is best for their needs.

When someone opens a bank account of any kind, he or she will be asked to provide certain identification and will need to give the bank a deposit, which is just another word for money in the form of cash or a check. That becomes the account balance. To add money to the account, the customer can make additional deposits at the bank, at an ATM, by mail, by transferring money from another account, or by having funds deposited electronically through a direct deposit. Employers use direct deposits to put paychecks directly into their employees' accounts.

TAKING MONEY OUT

So how can someone get money out of a bank account? Taking cash out of a bank account is called a withdrawal. Money in most bank accounts can be withdrawn directly through ATMs or by using paper withdrawal slips. To use a paper withdrawal slip, a customer must go to the bank during the hours it is open. An ATM card can be used to get cash from a

People with money in the bank can use an ATM to withdraw cash.

bank account even when the bank is closed. For a fee, most ATM cards can be used at other banks' ATMs, which is helpful if the customer's bank is not nearby.

Funds in a checking account can also be paid directly to another person. The old-fashioned way is by writing a check to someone to pay for something. But today, money can be transferred easily using online

CHECK IT OUT

In today's world, some bills must be paid by check. For example, people renting an apartment may have to write a rent check to their landlord. There are various steps to writing out a check. First, people need to fill in the date in the upper right-hand corner. Next, they have to write the name of the person or business they are paying on the "Pay to the Order of" line. Then, they should write the amount of the check in the box or on the line marked with the dollar sign. They also need to write the amount of the check in words, using a fraction for the cents on the dollar line and drawing a line to the end so no one can add anything. Finally, they have to sign the check in the lower right-hand corner. Before writing a check, it's always smart that people look at their bank account to see whether they can cover the cost.

banking linked to the bank account or by various phone apps. But debit cards are one of the most popular ways people make payments. A debit card, often combined with an ATM card, can be used at most stores. It electronically deducts money from a bank account and puts it into the store's bank account.

ON BALANCE

Bank accounts offer many conveniences. The smart way to manage a bank account is by keeping track of the balance that is in the account. This can be done through keeping a checking or savings account register. Registers are paper logs that a bank

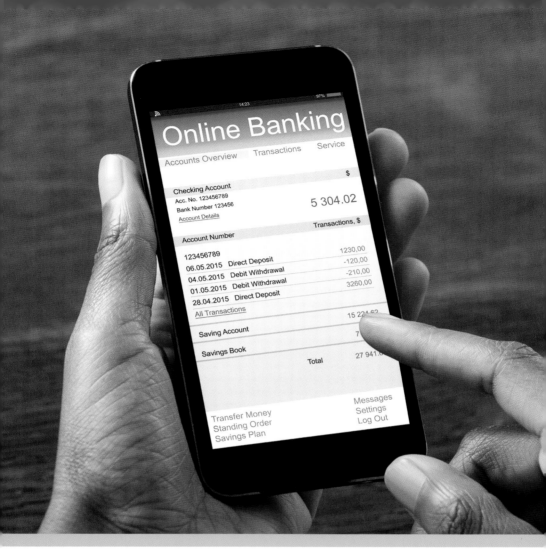

Technology can make looking at bank accounts easy.

gives a customer. The customer can fill in registers every time he or she makes a withdrawal, writes a check, or makes a deposit. The customer adds or subtracts the amount from the balance to know how much money is in the account. Many customers choose to look up the account at an ATM or online instead.

Either way, checking the balance is critical because if an account becomes overdrawn, meaning there isn't enough money to cover withdrawals or payments, the bank will charge fees. For example, if a young person has only $20 in his or her account but purchases a $25 item, the account will be overdrawn. The bank will then charge an overdraft fee. Overdraft fees vary depending on the bank. TCF Bank charges a $37 overdraft fee for each item.[3] Wells Fargo has an overdraft fee of $35.[4] It's good practice for teens to keep track of how much money is in their bank account and how much they are spending.

MONEY MATCHES

Making smart money choices means knowing the best places to keep your money. Depending on your financial goal, where would you keep your money? Put a check in each column where you think the money should go.

	Money for after-school snacks	Money for a video game	Money for college	Money for holiday gifts	Money for a monthly car payment
Wallet					
Piggy bank					
Savings account					
Checking account					

Explain your choices:

_____

_____

_____

_____

_____

_____

_____

_____

_____

_____

_____

_____

_____

_____

_____

_____

_____

_____

_____

_____

_____

_____

_____

_____

CHAPTER FIVE

THE ABCs OF BUDGETING

Creating a budget and planning for long-term purchases and goals are key strategies in smart money management. A budget is basically a compilation of a person's total income for the month minus his or her monthly savings, donations, and spending. Before starting, a person needs to figure out what style of budget works best for him or her. Some people use the envelope system. They keep their cash in different envelopes marked to identify what the money can be used for. Some people who are more tech savvy use a spreadsheet or budgeting software. But a common approach is to create a chart or list. Whichever approach, creating and sticking to a budget can help people make smart choices with their money.

Making a budget includes looking at all your expenses.

WHERE TEENS SPEND MONEY[1]

A 2017 report showed which items teens spent their money on.

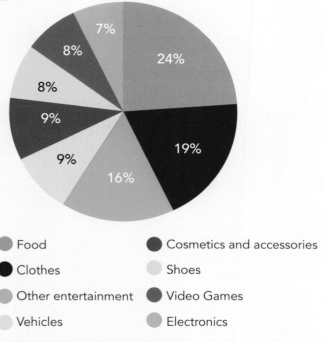

- 24%
- 19%
- 16%
- 9%
- 9%
- 8%
- 8%
- 7%

- ● Food
- ● Cosmetics and accessories
- ● Clothes
- ● Shoes
- ● Other entertainment
- ● Video Games
- ● Vehicles
- ● Electronics

HOW TO START

People can start their budget by tracking their expenses for one month. They should think about where their money goes. Do they pay for their own lunches or their portion of the family's cell phone bill?

Do they go to the movies several times a month? Do they buy clothes or other personal items, such as makeup, from time to time?

People should think about how often they buy these items. If they buy something at least once a month, they should include it in the list. Eating out or getting coffee regularly can also add up. For example, three $3 coffees a week adds up to about $36 per month. And a person who has a car should list all car-related expenses, such as gas, insurance, or a car loan payment. For some people, it can be hard to recall how they spend their money. If they have trouble remembering, they can try keeping an expense diary for a week or two. They should write down everything they spend money on.

Next, people should estimate their monthly income. They should include their allowance, routine payment for chores, money earned from neighborhood jobs, and paid employment after taxes. If people often sell things, such as crafts or baked goods, they should include their average net income from these sales. People shouldn't include the occasional gift or reward that comes once or twice a year. Then, they can add everything up to discover their net monthly income.

Finally, they can group their spending into categories such as food, clothing, transportation, and

MONEY AND TECHNOLOGY

As young people move away from home, they start paying bills such as rent, car loans, insurance, and utilities. People can pay bills in several ways. The old-fashioned way is to pay by check—a person simply writes a check and mails it in. Another way is to pay online. And a pre-authorized automated debit is a little different; it means that a person has given permission to a company, such as a cell phone provider, to withdraw money automatically from an account each month.

entertainment. They can add up how much they spend in each category. If people save money or donate money each month to a charity, they can add those to their list of expenses. Then, they should add up all of their expenses and be sure to calculate them on a monthly basis.

BALANCING ACT

Once people have their monthly income and monthly expenses, they can begin to create a budget. They should list their income in one column and total it. Then, they can list the expenses they've identified in another. People should keep their goals in mind. Some financial experts strongly recommend saving enough money to cover living expenses for three to six months. People should also consider setting up a rainy-day stash, but they should keep in mind that it should be used for emergencies they can't predict, not those that they should have seen coming. Once this is done, people should add up all their expenses, including additional saving and donating, and subtract this amount from their total income. If the amount left is zero, they have a balanced budget. But if the amount is less than zero, they don't have enough income to pay for their expenses. They will need to tweak their expenditures until they do.

What should a budget look like? Many people with families or who are living on their own use the 50-30-20 rule. That means one-half of their income should be spent on needs, such as food, clothes, and housing, 30 percent on wants, and 20 percent on savings.[2] But for those living at home, personal finance blogger Tamsen Butler suggests a 10 percent emergency fund

COMPARISON SHOPPING

When figuring out how to spend limited money, comparing just the price doesn't necessarily get people the best deal. For instance, if a candy bar costs $1 and a pack of five costs $4, which is the better deal? The unit price of a single bar is $1, but the unit price of a bar in the five-pack is $4 divided by five, or $0.80. Of course, if a person knows he's only going to eat one candy bar, it makes sense to buy only one.

and savings of between 10 and 40 percent of income, leaving the rest of the income available for spending on items such as clothes, activities, and food.[3]

Everyone budgets and spends money differently. It's important that people make a budget that works for their situation in order to make the smartest money choices possible.

BIG BUDGETS

Budgets are not just for individuals. Governments and corporations have budgets too—but they are much larger than an individual's. The federal government's budget is proposed by the president. Under the Constitution, Congress must approve the budget. The government's income comes primarily from taxes. Its expenses are the cost of benefits and programs that help its citizens, as well as interest on loans. People might wonder whether the government's budget is balanced. Although it was balanced and even had a surplus in 2001, the government's 2018 budget wasn't balanced, which means that the government borrows money to meet its expenses. In fact, it had a deficit of $779 billion.[4]

KEEPING ON BUDGET

Once people have a workable budget, they should keep it handy so they can monitor their actual spending. A good budget strategy is to compare income and expenses for a few weeks or months. If people find that they are regularly spending more in one area, they

Making a balanced budget can help people make smart choices about what to do with their money.

can decide whether they want to adjust their budget or their spending. Once people have a budget that fits, they should try to stick to it.

Sometimes it's not easy to follow a budget. Overspending, which is spending more than a person has allotted for a category in a budget, is a concern among teens. One pitfall is online spending. Retailers offer a wide array of merchandise that can be delivered quickly—sometimes even the next day. And purchasing takes just a couple of mouse clicks and a debit card. This is a great convenience, but it can be too easy to buy things a person doesn't need or hasn't saved up for. For example, if someone has already spent his monthly budget for clothes, he should probably not click "add to cart" for another pair of jeans.

It's also easy for people to give in to peer pressure and spend money they can't afford to spend. If a person's budget allows him or her only one fast-food meal a week, he or she could think of polite ways to resist peer pressure to go out more often. After someone has done the hard part in setting money limits, the smart thing to do is to spend within them.

SAVING STRATEGIES

In addition to having an emergency fund, people should determine any extra amount they want to save each month. A smart savings strategy for people is to list money they want to save before other spending and deduct it from their income first. This is what financial experts call "paying yourself first."[5] It means that people should list the amount they want to save as an expense. They can create a separate category for short-term savings in a budget. For example, if a person wants to save up for the latest gaming system, he should note that on his budget. It's also a smart idea for people to create a long-term savings category for really big items, such as cars and college.

The convenience of online shopping can lead people into making bad money choices.

In setting and tweaking savings goals, it's best practice to select goals that are attainable. For example, if a person earns $80 per month with a goal to save $70 a month yet likes to go to movies often, that savings goal is not attainable.

Goals should also be realistic and relevant to each person's lifestyle. And when people find that they don't have enough money to meet all their goals, they should either look for additional ways to earn money—perhaps an after-school job—or ways to reduce their spending, such as perhaps only one movie a month.

WEEKLY EXPENSES REPORT

Use this template to track your weekly expenses. Find patterns in your expenses.

	Food	Transportation costs (such as gas)	Personal care (such as clothing)
Monday			
Tuesday			
Wednesday			
Thursday			
Friday			
Saturday			
Sunday			
Total			

What do you spend your money on? What are some categories that you could cut back on to save money?

_____

_____

_____

_____

_____

Entertainment	Electronics	Miscellaneous

CHAPTER SIX

BIG PURCHASES

Some expensive items, including cars, computers, and cell phones, have become necessities for many teens. Teens can research a number of issues before making big purchases. This research can lead to more-informed decisions and better money choices.

START YOUR ENGINES

Safety is the first concern in any car purchase for a teen driver. Teenagers are inexperienced and much more likely to be involved in serious accidents. In fact, in the United States the number of fatal crashes for 16- to 19-year-olds is nearly three times the rate for drivers ages 20 and older.[1] The Insurance Institute for Highway Safety recommends, among other things, avoiding cars with high horsepower engines. It also recommends choosing larger, heavier cars. It lists the safest models of cars in different categories. The National Highway Traffic Safety Administration maintains a searchable

Purchasing a car is a big expense. Potential car buyers should keep in mind other expenses that come along with owning a car, including gas and maintenance.

website where car buyers can check the safety rating of a car of any make or model.

New cars come with a warranty—a promise that the manufacturer will replace or repair certain car parts if they break. Used cars are not usually covered by the warranty and may need expensive repairs. But under a warranty, the owner is still responsible for paying for routine maintenance such as oil changes and tire rotation. And cars need gas or electricity to run, which is another cost of car ownership.

Used cars are less expensive than new cars. But they still cost a lot. So how do people pay for them? Some people pay cash. They budget carefully, save up their money,

ACCOUNTS FOR SPECIFIC EXPENSES

After the Great Depression in the 1930s, Christmas club accounts became popular. They had nothing to do with a club—they were simply short-term savings accounts used to save up for holiday spending. The account holder couldn't withdraw money until a specific date close to the winter holiday season. Some banks, and even some stores, still offer these accounts, but they aren't as popular. However, the idea of a savings account set up for a specific purchase, such as a car, is still a good one.

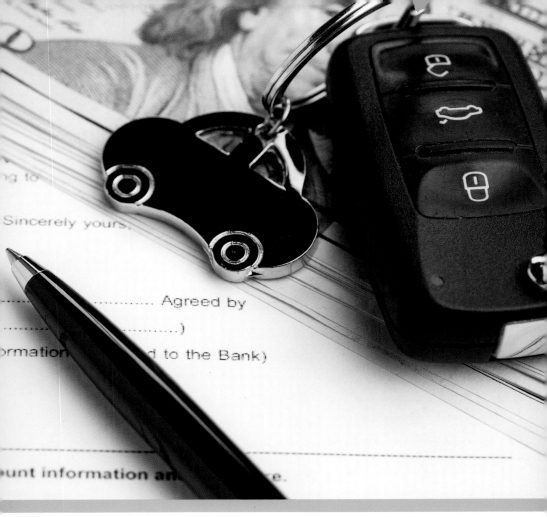

Taking out a car loan is a big financial decision for teens to make.

and purchase the car without taking out a loan. But many people can save up enough only for a down payment. A down payment is the amount of money the purchaser pays before taking out a loan. Some car dealers will sell a car with a very small down payment. But because cars don't maintain their value, experts recommend that car buyers put at least 20 percent down.[2] That way, people don't end up owing more

than the car is worth after a short time. The rest of the price is taken out in the form of a car loan. This is called financing. Banks and car dealerships offer car loans. Car loans must be paid back monthly with interest. Not all car loan payments will have equal amounts of monthly interest. Some people pay more interest at the start of their loan. It can take years to pay a car loan back. If a buyer fails to make payments, the bank or dealership can repossess and take back the car.

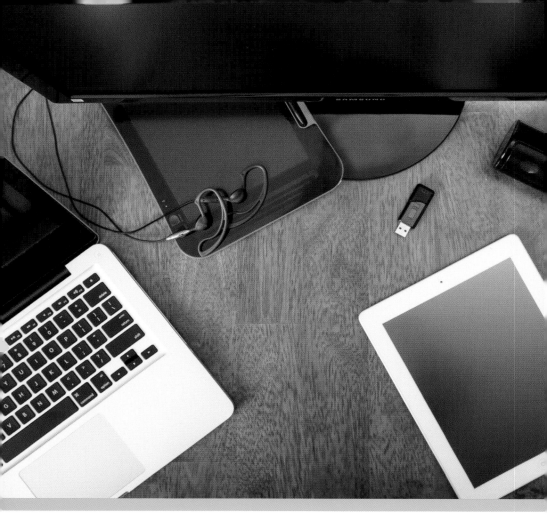

Teens should think carefully about which electronics they want to spend money on.

These phones are not tied to a carrier and are generally sold unlocked, which gives the owner flexibility about choosing a plan. Researching all the options will help people to make smart decisions.

COST OF A CAR LOAN

Financing a car will cost more in the long run than paying the purchase price in cash. That's because of interest rates. Also, people are supposed to make monthly payments on their loan. How much more would a car cost with a loan?

Figure it out for a car that costs $12,595. To finance the car, the dealer wants $2,500 as a down payment. The loan will have a monthly payment of $225 for 60 months (five years).

1. First, take the amount of the monthly payment and multiply it by the number of payments to be made over the term of the loan.

_____

2. Add that to the down payment ($2,500). This is the cost of the financed car.

_____

3. Now subtract the advertised cost of the car. The difference is what the loan cost.

_____

CHAPTER SEVEN

HOW CAN YOU BORROW MONEY WISELY?

ost people borrow money at some point during their lives. After all, that's how banks stay in business. Before taking out a loan, it's important for people to understand exactly how much they're borrowing and how the lender expects them to repay it. Some of the most common loans people take out are car loans, home loans, student loans, and payday loans.

CAR AND HOME LOANS

Money borrowed to purchase a car is called an installment loan. Most car loans are paid back within the course of a few years. The term, or length of the

Millions of Americans take out student loans to pay for college.

repayment period, is set when the money is borrowed. The loan is paid back in equal monthly installments. Home loans are usually called mortgages. They can be used to purchase a home or to make home improvements. Mortgages are usually paid back over a longer period of time—15 or 30 years. A smart choice, according to some finance experts, is to keep a mortgage payment to 28 percent or less of monthly gross (pretax) income.[1] That will leave enough money for other necessary expenses.

Car and home loans have something in common—they are secured loans. That means that they are tied to the property the money is being borrowed to purchase. And it means that if the borrower fails to make payments, the car can be repossessed, or taken back, and the house can be foreclosed, or sold, by the bank. Because they are for a set amount, car and home loans are closed-end loans.

OTHER TYPES OF CREDIT

In addition to car loans, home loans, and student loans, banks also lend money to small businesses and large corporations. And banks and stores also lend money through credit cards. That's why consumers have to get approval to get store and credit cards.

When the amount borrowed, or principal, is paid off, with interest, the loan ends.

STUDENT LOANS

Student loans are unsecured loans. They are not tied to, or backed by, tangible property, such as a car or house. But banks assume that with a college education, young people will make more money than without one and therefore will have enough to pay back the loan. Because these loans are not secured by actual property, they are a little riskier for the bank. The bank can't take a house or car if the debt isn't paid. But not paying back student loans hurts a person's credit score. Also, if a

CREDIT SCORE

A credit score is like a grade in the financial world. It's a three-digit number that tells banks and other lenders whether a person is a good risk for a future loan. There are several companies that collect and analyze a person's financial history to determine his or her credit score. These companies examine payment history, outstanding balances, how long the person has had credit, how many other new credit cards the person has, and the types of other debt the person has. Getting a credit card and paying it on time and in full will build a good credit history and earn a person a good credit score. Although a perfect score is 850, with many credit score companies any score over 700 is considered good or excellent.

person doesn't pay back his or her federal student loans, the government can take money out of his or her paycheck.

According to the US government, between 2009 and 2017, student borrowing doubled. And according to another government survey from 2016, 30 percent of all adults borrowed money to help pay for their education.[2] Some experts advise against borrowing more for an education than the student's expected annual salary at graduation.

PAYDAY LOANS

Payday loans are another type of unsecured loan. Getting a payday loan is not a savvy money choice. Independent lenders, such as storefront loan stores, generally make these types of loans instead of banks. And they are often established to take advantage of people.

Payday loans are loans to help someone pay bills until his or her next paycheck comes. Then the loan must be repaid, along with interest and fees. These are usually short-term loans for small amounts of money. But the interest and fees are very high—if calculated over a year, the interest can be 400 percent.[3] Payday loans are dangerous for consumers because borrowers can get behind every week and then end up spending

Getting a payday loan can be a risky choice.

hard-earned money on high interest. Many states have limited or even outlawed these loans.

LOANS FROM DIFFERENT SOURCES

Loans made by banks are regulated by federal and state governments to ensure that extensive information about the cost of the loan is provided to borrowers. For example, laws such as the Truth-in-Lending Act are designed to make sure that consumers know what is expected of them when they borrow money from a bank and how much they will have to repay. Other laws and regulations limit the amount of fees and interest a bank can charge. But there are people who will make loans outside of the system. They are sometimes called loan sharks because they are predators who will charge high interest rates. It's best not to get involved with them.

Who else can people borrow money from? Sometimes family members or friends will offer to help out with a loan. This can be a great way to get low- or no-interest money. But beware. Family and friend relationships can become strained or even broken when loans

STORE CREDIT

Some stores that sell expensive items, such as appliances and big-screen TVs, will finance purchases on a store credit card to convince a customer to buy the item. Sometimes there is no interest for the first few months. But afterwards, the interest rate is high—often 25 percent or more.[4] For example, a person might buy a $600 television and finance the entire amount at 18 percent interest. The monthly payment could be as low as $15, but it will take 5.2 years to pay it off. The interest would be $323, and the total cost of the television would be $923. Also, if a store offers six months free financing and the product is not paid in full within six months, the customer owes back interest from the start of the loan.

People need to pay off their credit card charges to avoid debt.

are involved, especially if the terms are not spelled out clearly at the start.

CHARGE IT

When people find items they want to buy, they have the option of putting the payment on a credit card. This can come in handy. For instance, if a person has been saving for a dress and then finds one on sale, she might want to buy it even though she doesn't have the money to pay for the entire purchase at the moment. She anticipates that by the time she gets the monthly bill, she'll have the rest of the money saved.

But what if people don't have enough money when the bill comes and they can't pay for the purchase?

DEBIT CARD VS. CREDIT CARD

Credit cards and debit cards look alike. Both options allow people to buy things from stores and online. But they're not the same thing. In general, debit cards are tied to bank accounts and the money is immediately withdrawn. Debit cards also allow people to withdraw cash from the account at a bank or ATM. People pay overdraft fees if they try to take out more money than is in the account. Credit cards are a form of borrowing. The person is spending the credit card company's money. It must be paid back as the monthly credit card bill. Failure to pay the bill on time can lead to additional fees and interest.

They are required to pay a minimum amount, but they also have the option of letting some of the balance carry over into the next month. That's how trouble starts. The balance becomes a loan. Credit card companies charge interest, often at high rates, on unpaid balances. When balances keep carrying over, credit card debt can quickly spiral out of control. For this reason, it is important to always pay off the full credit card bill every month.

Credit cards offer a great convenience. Some young people start with prepaid credit cards. These are sort of like gift cards that can be used anywhere. The teenager puts a certain amount of money on the card up front. It can be replenished, but the card can't be used if the

CHARGE CARDS TO CREDIT CARDS

In the early 1900s, stores began offering customers something called a charge card. These cards allow customers to purchase items in the store without cash, so long as they pay the balance on the card within a month. In the 1950s, companies such as American Express launched charge cards that weren't tied to any store and could be used at a number of different places. But these still had to be paid in full every month. But in 1958, Bank of America offered customers the BankAmericard—the first credit card and what would become a Visa card. Unlike the American Express charge card, the balance on a credit card does not have to be paid off in full every month. Instead, the balance accumulates interest.

balance is less than the purchase price. Young people may also choose a secured credit card. It's similar to a prepaid card, but the money paid in advance is refundable. It's just there for the bank to use in case the borrower doesn't pay the bill. People 18 and older can get their own non-prepaid cards. Younger teens usually have to have a parent agree to be responsible for charges if the teenager doesn't pay. Credit cards are a good way to learn about managing money and can be helpful in an emergency. Some credit cards offer cash back and frequent-flier airline miles based on how much is charged. But many charge annual fees, and all will charge steep interest rates on unpaid balances.

INTERESTED IN INTEREST?[5]

The annual percentage rate (APR) is what banks charge on credit card balances. A bank calculates how much interest is owed not just based on what you owe at the end of the monthly billing cycle but based on the average that was owed each day throughout the month. Do the math below to see just how quickly the interest adds up. Assume the APR is 11 percent.

1. To find out your daily rate, divide the APR by 365—the number of days in each year. _____

2. Assume you've spent $500 on your credit card by the first day in the month. Then, 15 days later, you spend another $500. You make no other purchases that month. What's your average balance for each day? To find this, the first step is to multiply the two balances ($500 and $1,000) by 15—which is the number of days you had each balance—and add the totals together. _____

3. Now, take the total from #2 and divide it by 30, which is the length of the month. That will give you your average daily balance. _____

4. To find how much interest you'll be charged, take the total from #3 and multiply it by the total from #1. Then, take that total and multiply it by 30. Move the decimal place two places to the left.

5. Total: _____

CHAPTER EIGHT

SHARING MONEY IN A SMART WAY

n 2015, psychologist Elizabeth Dunn studied the physical effects on people who donated money to charities. She found that giving money not only helps people in need but also can help the person making the donation. According to Dunn, she learned that giving to charity is "not just heartwarming, it may be quite literally good for our hearts."[1] That's because donating to charity actually lowers the giver's blood pressure.

FIND THE RIGHT CHARITY

If donating to charity is important to a person, it makes sense to give it high priority on the list of monthly expenses in a budget. Before donating, however, it's important to look for an organization that helps

People can donate money online, but they should be careful to contribute to a reputable organization.

Donating food and water after a disaster can help many people.

T-shirt giveaways. Running these events and giving away merchandise can eat up a fair percentage of the money raised. This, in turn, reduces the amount of money that actually goes to the cause—sometimes by almost 20 percent.[2] But there are ways to check out an organization. People should research the specific charity online and learn about how it operates. And it's a smart idea to go to websites such as Charity Watch and Charity Navigator before giving. These organizations give charities scores or rankings based on how they use their donations.

Some nonprofit organizations use hard-sell tactics. It's important for people to resist getting pushed into charitable giving beyond their comfort zone. And some people operate scams. These fake charities are

YOUNG PEOPLE MAKING A DIFFERENCE

People are never too young to start doing good things—and that includes founding charitable organizations. A number of children who saw needs that were not being taken care of have done just that. Hannah Taylor was just five years old when she saw a man without a home eating from a garbage can. When she was eight, she took action and founded the Ladybug Foundation to help people who are homeless. This Canadian charity has raised millions of dollars as of 2018. The money is given to existing organizations that provide things such as food and shelter to homeless people.

particularly common online. One popular scam is an email or message on social media about someone who is in a dangerous situation or has a terrible illness and needs money right away. Some online donation requests, like those made through GoFundMe, are monitored. Fund-raisers that set up donations through these types of organizations are usually trustworthy. But scam operations can slip through. Sometimes, people fake an illness or fabricate other problems to try to get money. To be a smart giver, it pays to research the charity first. Reading about an organization's mission, operations, budget, and leadership helps people make smart donation choices.

RESEARCHING CHARITIES

Look up five charities that match your interests and passions on either Charity Watch or Charity Navigator and determine their charity score.

Name of charity	Charity score	Would you donate to this charity based on its score? Why or why not?

CHAPTER NINE

AVOIDING MISTAKES AND SCAMS

A s young people enter the world of finance, they need to be smart about protecting their money. Thieves can steal credit cards and identities, and scammers can take money and not deliver what was promised in return. Some cons are targeted at young people. Scammers use false advertising, false job offers, and fake prizes to steal money.

WHERE'S MY CARD?

People tend to panic if they lose their credit or debit card. The best way to avoid losing these cards is to keep them in the same safe place all the time. It sounds easy, but it's also easy when someone is in a rush to stick the card in a different pocket or place it in a purse and then panic when it can't be found later.

Chips make credit and debit cards more secure. This means that it's more difficult for hackers to steal the cards' data.

And it is smart to double-check the tray or plastic envelope that comes with a restaurant check to make sure no cards are left behind after the bill is signed.

It's also advisable not to lend a card to anyone. It can get lost or misused. And people should use cards online only at trusted sites. Online hackers can steal financial information very quickly with just a small amount of information. And they can use it to buy expensive items charged to other people's accounts.

TOO GOOD TO BE TRUE

The Federal Trade Commission (FTC), an agency of the US government, regulates advertising. According to the FTC, an ad in print, on TV, or on the internet must be truthful. Not only must an ad not contain lies; it can't be misleading, either. And when possible, ads should be backed by scientific evidence. For example, an ad that says a brand of hot dogs is the best is OK—this claim is just an opinion, so the company doesn't need to provide hard scientific evidence for it. But if the ad says that the product is made from a particular ingredient, the company is making a specific factual claim. If the product does not contain that ingredient, the company is lying—a practice known as false advertising. False advertising is often convincing.

Times Square in New York City has many different advertisements.

People should be savvy and double-check items before purchasing them so they are not misled by ads. If people educate themselves on products before buying them, they can avoid throwing away their money on a product they don't want. If the ad sounds too good to be true, it probably is.

EXAMPLES OF SCAMS

Someone stops a person in the mall and tells the person he or she has the right look to be a model or an actor. And maybe the person does. Perhaps this person

WHEN SOMETHING BAD HAPPENS

Sometimes bad things happen, even if people are careful. A debit or credit card may be lost or stolen. If a person loses her card, she should report it to her bank immediately. The bank will block the account so no one can use it. And if someone has used the card to buy things before the bank was notified, federal law limits the amount the cardholder will have to pay for the purchases made illegally to $50.[1]

Another danger is identity theft, especially if a card is used online. Hackers can break into online stores' databases, which may store information about people who shop there, and find people's credit card information. The hackers then try to use the person's credit cards. People are also at risk of identity theft when using free Wi-Fi. Hackers can steal information if they're using the same internet connection.

Here are a few smart tips people can follow to reduce the risk: use strong passwords to make it harder for hackers to break in, buy things only from websites that begin with https—the "s" indicates that the website is secure—and monitor accounts frequently. And if anything suspicious shows up on a debit or credit card bill, the cardholder must call the bank right away.

is a talent scout who knows what the market is looking for and can find the person a modeling job. But people should be cautious because fake offers for jobs such as modeling and acting are common and targeted at young people.

Teenagers often take the person's business card or phone number and show up at the designated time and place for an interview. But when the teen gets there, he or she sees that the office is overflowing with other young people. And when finally interviewed, the young person is pressured for money for photographs and screen tests. And the scout wants the money in full, up front, and in cash.

This is a scam. And any claims that the money is fully refundable are usually overstated because the conditions for a refund are usually strictly limited. Modeling and acting agents that are legitimate don't conduct business this way. Agents get paid only when they find people work. And they ask people to bring photographs, called head shots, taken by a photographer the person chose. Schools for acting and modeling ask teens to sign up for lessons for a fee and then provide instruction. They may offer help in placement upon completion, but

TAKE IT BACK

People sometimes buy items, get them home, and discover that they don't fit in the space, don't match other things, or just don't look as good as they did in the store. Sometimes people realize that the money they spent should have been saved for a different purchase—a feeling sometimes called buyer's remorse. There's good news: most items can be returned or exchanged. But check the receipt or call the store for details on return policies. Often returns must be made within a certain number of days, be accompanied by the receipt, and sometimes have the original tags on them.

PONZI SCHEMES

A Ponzi scheme is a fraudulent investment scheme. In a Ponzi scheme, one person collects money from investors and uses the money to pay interest to other investors, keeping part for himself. But usually there's no real investment, so eventually the scheme falls apart. By then, the person who started it has made a lot of money. This type of fraud was named after Charles Ponzi, who conned people with a postage-stamp investment scheme in the 1920s. People still fall for similar schemes. In 2009, businessman Bernie Madoff was convicted of running one. He stole $65 billion from investors and was sent to prison.[2]

it's up to the student to find work. These are legitimate ways to break into the modeling and acting fields. But agents and schools aren't generally in malls searching for clients. In fact, anyone who asks to be paid a fee before hiring someone is not usually legitimate, so people should be wary before handing over any money.

WINNING A FREE TRIP

The county fair, the mall, and trade shows are all places where booths can be set up to offer people the chance to win a "free" trip. A person signs up and then gets a call. Sometimes people get random calls even without having signed up. The telemarketer

People should never give their credit card number to a telemarketer over the phone.

tells them that they've won a free trip. But to get it, they need to give the telemarketer a credit card to set up an account. And then the telemarketer explains all the additional fees the person is responsible for. This "win" is probably not legitimate. And the consumer can end up paying a fortune for a trip that is anything but free.

Some free trips actually involve going somewhere. And that's because once the person arrives at the destination, he or she must sit through a long sales presentation about some property or vacation club that is for sale, and the person must be old enough to sign a contract. People can say "no" and just enjoy the free vacation—but the sales pitch could be hard to resist.

Everyone has the ability to make smart money choices that will help them financially in the long run. People can find ways to increase their earnings, research and understand fully how banks work, create a budget and commit to sticking to it, do research before buying expensive items and taking out loans, and watch out for scams. Each of these things will create a money-smart consumer.

LOOK CRITICALLY
AT ADVERTISEMENTS

Study and analyze three advertisements you see in the media, such as on billboards, on TV, or on the internet. After looking at the advertisements critically, do you think they are credible?

	Advertisement 1	Advertisement 2	Advertisement 3
What is the topic of the ad?			
What claims does the ad make?			
Are the claims factual or opinion based?			
Does the ad support its claims? If so, how?			
Does the ad seem credible?			

KEY TAKEAWAYS

TOP 10 MOST IMPORTANT CONCEPTS

1. Overspending happens when people don't have a mechanism to keep track of their spending.

2. It's important for people to recognize the difference between needs and wants and to evaluate wants by determining the opportunity cost.

3. Setting up a budget is a great way for people to manage their money and to save for their goals.

4. Teens can find a number of ways to get extra money, such as doing extra chores, getting a part-time or summer job, working for neighbors, and selling things they make.

5. Consider "paying yourself first" by making saving a priority. Savings accounts at banks can make this easier.

6. Teens can open bank accounts that offer debit cards, which are handy when shopping because they immediately deduct money from the accounts.

7. Credit cards might be convenient, but carrying a balance from month to month can lead to high interest rates and credit card debt.

8. Car loans are costly, so it's best to save up as much money as possible before buying a car.

9. Teens are often targeted by scammers, so they should be wary of false advertising, identity theft, fake job offers, and offers of free trips.

10. If people want to give money to charity, they should find an organization that inspires them and is legitimate.

TOP 5 TAKEAWAYS

1. Make a budget.

2. Open a bank account.

3. Find ways to increase your income.

4. Keep track of and try to limit your spending.

5. Find a way to share your time or money with others.

GLOSSARY

balance
The amount of money in an account.

credit
A person's ability to get services or goods before making a payment, based on the belief that he or she will make a payment in the future.

credit history
A person's history of paying bills.

deficit
An economic state when more money has been spent than has been made.

deposit
To put money into an account at a bank.

down payment
Money paid up front when purchasing something on credit; the payment is usually a percentage of the total cost of the item.

entrepreneur
A person who organizes and operates a business or businesses.

installment
One of many payments made regularly over time for an object that was purchased.

insurance

Coverage people pay for in case they experience a loss, such as that from fire or flooding. The coverage gives people money to help replace what was damaged or destroyed.

interest

A fee charged when a person or business borrows money, or money paid to people as an incentive for keeping their money in a bank.

mortgage

A legal agreement by which a bank or other creditor lends money at interest in exchange for taking title of the debtor's property.

net income

Income after exemptions and deductions are made.

premium

Money paid toward an insurance policy.

ADDITIONAL RESOURCES

SELECTED BIBLIOGRAPHY

"Banking Supervision." *Federal Reserve Education*, n.d., federalreserveeducation.org. Accessed 10 Oct. 2018.

"FDIC Consumer News." *Federal Deposit Insurance Corporation*, Spring 2008, fdic.gov. Accessed 10 Oct. 2018.

"What Is a Money Market Account?" *Consumer Financial Protection Bureau*, 18 Mar. 2016, consumerfinance.gov. Accessed 10 Oct. 2018.

FURTHER READINGS

Butler, Tamsen. *The Complete Guide to Personal Finance for Teenagers and College Students*. Atlantic, 2016.

Edwards, Sue Bradford. *Earning, Saving, and Investing*. Abdo, 2020.

ONLINE RESOURCES

Booklinks
NONFICTION NETWORK
FREE! ONLINE NONFICTION RESOURCES

To learn more about making smart money choices, please visit **abdobooklinks.com** or scan this QR code. These links are routinely monitored and updated to provide the most current information available.

MORE INFORMATION

For more information on this subject, contact or visit the following organizations:

CHARITY NAVIGATOR
139 Harristown Road, Suite 101
Glen Rock, NJ 07452
charitynavigator.org
This website is a good place to research charitable organizations that people are interested in supporting.

FEDERAL TRADE COMMISSION (FTC)
600 Pennsylvania Avenue NW
Washington, DC 20580
202-326-2222
consumer.ftc.gov
The FTC gives information about credit and debit cards and works to protect consumers from fraud.

SOURCE NOTES

CHAPTER 1. EMPTY POCKETS

1. Mallory Schlossberg. "We Polled 110 Teenagers on Which Brands They Love and Hate in 2016." *Business Insider*, 3 July 2016, businessinsider.com. Accessed 26 Dec. 2018.

2. Jordan Wathen. "How Do Savings Bonds Work?" *Motley Fool*, 15 Apr. 2015, fool.com. Accessed 26 Dec. 2018.

3. "7 Reasons We Overspend (and How to Overcome Them)." *Popsugar*, 1 July 2013, popsugar.com. Accessed 26 Dec. 2018.

4. "Changes in US Family Finances from 2013 to 2016: Evidence from the Survey of Consumer Finances." *Federal Reserve*, Sept. 2017, federalreserve.gov. Accessed 26 Dec. 2018.

CHAPTER 2. NEEDS, WANTS, AND OPPORTUNITY COSTS

None.

CHAPTER 3. SMART WAYS TO GET MONEY

1. "The Kids Allowance Report—US." *Rooster Money*, n.d., roostermoney.com. Accessed 27 Dec. 2018.

2. "The Kids Allowance Report."

3. "The Kids Allowance Report."

4. Annie Nova. "Here's How Much the Typical Kid Gets in Allowance Each Year." *USA Today*, 9 Jan. 2018, usatoday.com. Accessed 27 Dec. 2018.

5. "Child Labor." *History*, n.d., history.com. Accessed 27 Dec. 2018.

6. "May 2017 National Occupational Employment and Wage Estimates United States." *Bureau of Labor Statistics*, n.d., bls.gov. Accessed 27 Dec. 2018.

7. "May 2017 National Occupational Employment and Wage Estimates United States."

CHAPTER 4. SMART PLACES TO KEEP MONEY

1. "Fidelity Fiduciary Bank." *YouTube*, 8 Aug. 2010, youtube.com. Accessed 27 Dec. 2018.

2. "Learning Bank—About the FDIC." *Federal Deposit Insurance Corporation*, n.d., fdic.gov. Accessed 27 Dec. 2018.

3. "What You Need to Know about Overdrafts and Overdraft Fees." *TCF Bank*, n.d., tcfbank.com. Accessed 27 Dec. 2018.

4. Margarette Burnette. "Wells Fargo Overdraft Fees and Policies." *Nerd Wallet*, 21 Nov. 2018, nerdwallet.com. Accessed 27 Dec. 2018.

CHAPTER 5. THE ABCs OF BUDGETING

1. Hayley Peterson. "Teens Have a New Favorite Restaurant— and It's Not Starbucks." *Business Insider*, 11 Apr. 2017, businessinsider.com. Accessed 27 Dec. 2018.

2. Paula Pant. "The 50/30/20 Rule of Thumb for Budgeting." *Balance*, 21 Dec. 2018, thebalance.com. Accessed 27 Dec. 2018.

3. Tamsen Butler. *The Complete Guide to Personal Finance for Teenagers and College Students*. Atlantic Publishing Group, 2016. 79.

4. Jim Tankersley. "Budget Deficit Jumps Nearly 17% in 2018." *New York Times*, 15 Oct. 2018, nytimes.com. Accessed 27 Dec. 2018.

5. "Special Edition: Money Tips for All Ages." *Federal Deposit Insurance Corporation*, Spring 2008, fdic.gov. Accessed 27 Dec. 2018.

CHAPTER 6. BIG PURCHASES

1. "Teenagers." *Insurance Institute for Highway Safety*, 2016, iihs.org. Accessed 27 Dec. 2018.

SOURCE NOTES CONTINUED

2. Jeanne Lee. "How Much Should My Car Down Payment Be?" *Nerd Wallet*, 9 Oct. 2015, nerdwallet.com. Accessed 27 Dec. 2018.

CHAPTER 7. HOW CAN YOU BORROW MONEY WISELY?

1. David Weliver. "What Percentage of Your Income Can You Afford for Mortgage Payments?" *Money Under 30*, 3 Oct. 2017, moneyunder30.com. Accessed 27 Dec. 2018.

2. "Education Debt and Student Loans." *Federal Reserve*, n.d., federalreserve.gov. Accessed 27 Dec. 2018.

3. Miriam Caldwell. "What Is a Payday Loan?" *Balance*, 26 Nov. 2018, thebalance.com. Accessed 27 Dec. 2018.

4. Satta Sarmah Hightower. "Credit Karma's Guide to Retail Credit Cards." *Credit Karma*, 4 Dec. 2018, creditkarma.com. Accessed 27 Dec. 2018.

5. Holly Johnson. "How Do You Calculate Credit Card Interest?" *Simple Dollar*, 30 May 2018, thesimpledollar.com. Accessed 27 Dec. 2018.

CHAPTER 8. SHARING MONEY IN A SMART WAY

1. Joseph D'Urso. "Giving to Charity Makes You Happy, Middle Age Is Miserable: Experts." *Reuters*, 4 Sept. 2015, reuters.com. Accessed 27 Dec. 2018.

2. Jim Probasco. "Where Does My United Way Money Go." *Love to Know*, n.d., charity.lovetoknow.com. Accessed 27 Dec. 2018.

CHAPTER 9. AVOIDING MISTAKES AND SCAMS

1. Stan Murray. "Who Is Liable for Credit Card Fraud?" *Investopedia*, 22 May 2018, investopedia.com. Accessed 27 Dec. 2018.

2. Stephanie Yang. "5 Years Ago Bernie Madoff Was Sentenced to 150 Years in Prison—Here's How His Scheme Worked." *Business Insider*, 1 July 2014, businessinsider.com. Accessed 27 Dec. 2018.

INDEX

INDEX CONTINUED

ABOUT THE AUTHOR

Moira Rose Donohue was a banking lawyer for almost 20 years, working at both banks and federal bank regulatory agencies, before finding the greater joy of writing for children. She has published more than 25 books for children, with more on the way. She now lives in Saint Petersburg, Florida, with her devoted dog, Petunia.

ABOUT THE CONSULTANT

Dr. Linda Simpson, PhD, CFCS, CPFFE, has been a faculty member in the School of Family and Consumer Sciences at Eastern Illinois University since 1997. She has been the founder and executive director of the Literacy in Financial Education (LIFE) Center. The purpose of the center is to prepare college students to play an active role in managing their personal finances and make informed decisions about saving, spending, and borrowing. Based on the educational programs developed for the center, Dr. Simpson received the 2016 Family Economics and Resource Management Community Award from the Community of Family Economics and Resource Management of the American Association of Family and Consumer Sciences.

Dr. Simpson received a PhD from the University of Illinois and MS and BS degrees from Eastern Illinois University. She has numerous publications and has presented at conferences on the topics of online teaching and learning, budgeting and debt management, and consumer behavior.